BURNING OFF THE DEADWOOD

by Tracy Downs

Cover art by Marisa Olvera

Published in the United States of America.
ISBN 979-8-360-88621-1

Introduction

I have to say these poems do not really reflect who I am now, but they are legitimate representations of who I was when I wrote them, and of things I was going through at different stages in my life. Things that, no doubt, others have been and are now going through. So I offer them to you in a spirit of solidarity, of empathy.

I put this book out now as a way of burning off the deadwood of my old life, burning off the deadwood in myself – releasing it as part of the process of moving forward, in my writing and in my days. It is an act which brings to completion a long period of change and healing, and starts a new one. As long as we are on this earth, we are not finished.

I have found a new life far removed from all the anxieties and troubles of my former life, so I believe that is possible for everyone.

May you too find healing and peace.

For Brian

Table of Contents

DIGGING UP A LIFE

Loving you
Is a skill I have developed.
Like speaking Latin,
An obsolete skill.
A dead language.
The angry buzzing of bees.

Like last year's pomegranates
Clinging stiffly to the branch,
Like a wife who won't go away.
Hollow as a sterile womb.
Bent and fragile
Like last season's fennel.

The new growth beneath
Feathery and supple.
Under the decay, fighting for life.
Acid thoughts burn my brain
Synapses no longer firing.
Dead batteries, foggy mornings.

Not enough alprazolam in the world
To calm this wounded animal.
I emote like a panther
Pacing my empty cage.
The sorrow is not dissipated,
But rather multiplies.

I have collected the tears
Like a thousand crystal trophies
Awarded to your decision.
Where are you God?
I keep calling
But no one answers.

All the earth's aloneness
Dwells within the
Fragments of my heart.
I gave away all the trees
To someone
who still had hope.

The white pine should not have to suffer
Because you stopped loving me.
They were so happy:
"Our first tree", she said,
And I felt the haunting.
The ghost of our first tree.

I wanted to scream "Run!
He'll leave when you least expect it;
You'll have nothing left
but this tree".
Some Dysentra
has gone to happy home.

A million Bleeding Hearts
left in the yard,
Swaying in the breeze
Echoing their sorrow to my own.
I dug up the rosebushes.
"Take them", I said.

They are no good to me now,
Without love.
Let them go somewhere
Where hearts still beat.
I am emptied.
A hollow drum.

All my books are in boxes.
Their knowledge, the shiny pictures.
Even the theologians
Folded up against one another
Like lovers.
Like we once slept, flesh against flesh.

Eventually to come away empty.
Flat pages with nothing to say
White and dead like paper.
Even the memories are ghosts now,
Appearing suddenly, rising like pain
In the hollow of my heart.

DARK SECRET

I am buying silence
Paying in feathers
And smooth colored stones.

I have lit many candles
Asked for guidance.

I have walked
In blood red light
On a desert highway.

I have written
A chapter on sadness
Then closed the book
And sealed the door.

I have spoken to no one
Touched nothing
Felt naught.
I have painted a color
You cannot see.

I have hung my door
In garlic and barbed wire,
Gaping wounds and crucifixes.

Erase my name from the book.
Tear down the mailbox.
Turn the mirrors to the wall.

Burn the television, the phone.
Throw the computer in the street.
Give me only silence.

ESCAPE

What is this love –
This terrible love?
Its acid fruits sparking fires –
How we burn.

Fragile bones of my feet
Tread gingerly the wall
Between pick up your cross
And summon my inner warrior.

Too dangerous it seems
To fall to either side.

Mouth full of barbed wire
I dive to the deep
Fingers grasping a tangle
Of dark roots.
I resolve to stay here.

Self-preservation instinct
Too strong.
Kicking and screaming
I rise to the surface
I breathe...I breathe.

LA PIETA

The still sanctity of stone
Sacred Virgin
Mother of God
Cradling her broken son
Soothed by angels
Unseen.

Palms and feet bruised
And gashed
Skin pale with holiness
The piety of death.

Platonistic, quintessence
Of perfect love.
Image of death.
Model of life.

LOVE STORY

I picked you up
Long ago
Like broken glass
Sparkly, jagged
Glittering and dangerous.

I carried you
In my hands
For over twenty years.
On my guard like a sentry
At love's gate.

Separated, I wrote you daily.
The return address read:
Your king and your country.
You called at every sunset.
We mourned.

Like you were away on a battlefield
Instead of playing guitar
In some dive in Northern New Mexico.
Those were the good days
Submerged in love.

Now you lie under the grass
Under a stone
Bearing both our names.
Wait for me.
I will be there soon.

SEPTEMBER, WASHINGTON

The gull's scream
Liquid and silver
Like mercury.

The promise of
An unread book
And a soft blanket.

I live for this
The darkening day
The rains return.

CHARLIE BIRD

"Do you want a bird?"
She said.
"Sure."

As if it weren't loud enough,
We found him
A friend.

Now here we are
Covered in red and blue feathers
And fearful hope.

The birds whisper
Memories from someone
Else's life.

Their eventual love
A screaming, demanding
Obligation and duty.

As always,
Well-meaning,
and in over my head.

STARTING AGAIN, ANONYMOUSLY

She has washed
Her hands of it
Dried her eyes
Shed her blood.

She has altered
The lines of her palm
So as not to expose
The secret
Of her destiny.

FEAST DAY OF ST. MONICA

I can not fill this hole
With food or wine
Or tranquilizers.
No activity
Is numbing enough.

St. Monica pray for me.
I am a hollow drum
echoing endlessly
even the sound dissipates
bearing no fruit.

Anyone can have a baby.
God even gave babies
To women who killed them.
He had to have known
It was going to happen.

But I am empty
And nothing
Will grow inside me
Except tears and bitterness.
What future?

ON COMING HERE FROM SOMEPLACE DARK AND WARM

I am too thin for you people
Too frightened, too dangerous
You are loud noises
The bang of guns
Hatred.

You are the sun
Too bright for my eyes
I pick you off like fleas
Like glints of glass
At the edge of the highway.

I pick you off like a sniper
At noon rush
Bottles at a carnival arcade
Because I am too fragile
For you, people.

I am afraid of your turbulence
Your bad energy
Your steps are too loud
Your voices boom
Even your hands
Jump at me

I taste fear
In your mouths
I scratch
And claw the earth
Trying to get back inside

<u>THE CITY WILL HAVE IT'S WAY</u>

The mountains are black
But sparkle
Diamond-like
Where the city
Has spread
It's hungry talons
Reaching
Like jeweled
Pewter rivers
Flowing uphill

I REMEMBER

I have recorded
All your lies
Saved them
For possible future display
Like an incorrupt saint

I've put them
In a secure place
For now
With your promises

I have collected
All these things
Like a crazed magpie
Every lie
Every shiny object

But it's time now
To abandon them
Unseen, unspoken
In my private graveyard
Of dead poems and lost loves.

DOWNTOWN AFTER 9PM

The drunks are propped up
Around the city
Monuments to our wisdom
Road kill like sacrifices
On the altars of our streets
Bearing tribute
To our infinite humanity
Our progress.
The dogs are running around
Snarling at each other
So many dogs
I can't move my feet.
At the edge of consciousness
A man with black eyes
Waits.
Trading mom's silver
To the stealer of souls
Angel of death
With a green balloon.
Lurking silhouettes and shadows
Garbage tossed
By the cold impartial wind
Samurai bag lady
Near a man with gray skin
Waiting nervously
Waiting for the roaches
To go live somewhere else
Waiting for a shining presence

To remove the grime
Like some modern-day Mr. Clean
Waiting for some vague mystery
To be solved.
Waiting to understand
Waiting for things to be better.
Just waiting.

RECURRENT DREAM

She was a city
Of crystal streets
And fluid skies.

The sun rose
With great promise
And she shone
Brighter than any star.

Then men
Rushed in to break her up
With their long sticks –
Brutal weapons.

She awakens
Chewing broken glass
Spitting out fragments
Mouth bloodied.

FEAST OF THE HOLY INNOCENTS

Uterine madness.
We are separated by miles –
The great wall
Between lipstick and testosterone.

Decorated with breasts and thighs
But without biological purpose
I mourn the spirals of light
That might have been scientists or madmen.
Gynecological ghost town.

St. Monica help me
I have truly failed the God who sent us
To be fruitful and multiply.
I excel at failure, an accomplished storm
A blaze of wind leaving nothing behind.

My womb paper
An abandoned wasp's nest
Peel away the layers, the little bronze cubbies
Peel away the years, the tears
The fears and the good intentions.

Only a battered emptiness there
Like the skeleton of a house
Remaining in the desert
Someone's dream that died.
We've all thought we'd make a go of it.

A EULOGY FOR YOUTH

We are timeless tides
Stretched across the sea
Crashing and shrieking
For what could
But will not be.

We are dogs
After the hunt
Feeding on red and rich organs
Licking our wounds
In mourning
For dead guitarists
And what we
Used to call desire.

We are the last generation
And the first
Who have no home.

THE APPLE GOT THEM AGAIN

Turn off
The little sparkly gods
And awaken.

The same eye
That captures
The sunset

Can also ensnare
The one
Who adored it.

You treat it
Like an appendage.
A convenience.

It is a trap.
It is the noose
Around your neck.

It is the scent in the wind
They will follow.

AT PEACE

Here am I kneeling
Surrounded by wild beasts.
I am not afraid.
I am not anything.

I am like Eve in the garden
Or Mary in the stable.
But I will not do
Great good or great evil.

Only mediocrity –
Failing this person a little here
That person a little there.
Content in my lack of expectations.

I want to reach my roots
Deep into the soil
Draw nourishment
Minerals, water, hope.

The Scrub Jay watches me
And waits.
We exchange
Knowing glances.

I am happy today –
Surrounded by the beasts
Their feathers and fur
Honest and real.

I wake up in this magic place,
Undeserving. The dogs
Run wild figure eights
Around the yard.

Birds rest in the trees, despite
The propensity of the dogs
To chase them away.
Love fills the sky.

LIFE FORCE

A fog rolling off the abyss
Anonymously
Soothes the planet

Neither stone nor steel the powerful
Sculptor of earth
But a raindrop

Even the great lava flows
Carving deadly paths
Stop stunned at meeting the sea

The gaping red mouth
Choking, dying quickly
Without fanfare.

UP NORTH

It is black when I rise.
Black when I return
In evening.

Shadows
Woven into the dark tapestry
Of moldy winter.

Smell of wet dogs.
Fireplace smoke.
The North is savage.

No less I,
To remain sterile on this soil
so black and fecund.

Both mold and frost
Multiply prolifically on the panes
Like a bad omen.

You have brought me great joy
But your acorns
Will never give me an oak tree.

WING-ED

I am obsessing
About the ravens again.
My keyboard has one key
Repeat. Repeat. Repeat.

But look at them!
Their black swooping
Their sooty beauty
The primaries lifting at the edge.

The ravens settle to the ground
They are more than dancers
More than birds
They are astronauts.

They bring me celestial wonder
In their simple contentment.
They bring me bread and hope
Like Elijah in the Wadi Cherith.

WHEN YOUR HUSBAND IS IN A BOX

Poems, books – they are not trees
But they were once
When they were worthwhile.

Now I'd trade them all
For the cry of the red-tailed hawk
The sight of a cumulous cloud
Your breath on my neck
One last conversation
One last call
Forgiveness.

I'm sorry –
I thought we had more time
I was letting the healing
Come slowly, like soft rain
I wasn't ready to let it go
And then it was
Gone.

MARRIAGE #1

In the gloom
The television
Watches you.

Shadows and light
Dance
Across your face.

I wander the house
A ghost
Pale and silent.

THE PAINTING

Anyone could see it was evil
Droning, mechanical
Renaissance shades and tones

Ripping an obscure
No - invisible
Christ back off the cross.

I didn't want
To be in the room with it
Its black wasp buzzing.

It occupied the entire house
Crowding out
Perspective and reason.

A wise man finally
destroyed it. Too late though.
After the murder.

HERITAGE

I watched the body
Of my grandmother die
With very little emotion.
Her soul having left
Some time before.

Her skin already
Smelling of the grave
Cracking and decomposing.
I timed her breaths
In a clinical manner.

Only the second hand
Of my watch seemed rational,
bearable. The lighting was heartless
Blocking the warmth
of the sunlight from the window.

We all just sat there
In the shadow
Of the yawning grave.
And when death took her
Everyone embraced.

I smelled her
On all of them, as if death
were our family smell.
I heard the clacking of footsteps
Up and down the hall.

I knew God was there
But we never spoke of it.
Years later, she would come to me
in a dream. They didn't seem
to believe that either.

PATRIARCH

We were raised up
Like soldiers
Risen from the muck
Obedient
Proud soldiers
Bootstrap children
Holding the stiff upper lip
Holding ourselves
Like monuments
Raised to you.

Dear old Dad
Raised all his girls
To be men
Strong and unbending
Ruthless, unsatisfied
To love money
To win
Win
Win
Win.

CORVIDAE

In my dreams they are as large as condors
And they love me
Like one of their own.
They are life to me.
Stark feathered regal beauty.

I pass a congregation of crows
And cross myself instinctively.
I am in the presence of holiness.
These are God's crows
But he has charged me with their care.

I bury their dead, crying.
In the pouring rain
I bury their dead
Thinking we must have done
Some terrible thing.

And God is punishing us
With these terrible
Broken black bodies
Falling like rain
Into the yard.

Later, I hear the neighbor boy
Call out to his friend
"Let's go shoot some seagulls".
Vindication
And the end of hope.

IF YOU RETURN

From that place, far away
Where the stars reach down to the sea
Before I myself have departed
I will be waiting.

I have left instructions.
I have planned everything.
I chose a red granite
With a Celtic cross and two ravens.

The stone is ready and already placed.
Grass grows there.
Our names are spelled correctly.
I visit sometimes, and I hope.

INTUITIVE

I have walked by the water
And felt the spirits of drowned children
Ever trapped, struggling for breath
Grasping pink small hands

I have felt the grains of earth
Bones beneath my feet
Of those who have no tombs
The ones who met the wrong road one day

I have breathed the air
Odor of blood on the wind
Smell of fear and confusion
Of those who died without reason

I have heard the screams
Of the random chosen
Echoing across an empty field
Of victims, of would-be victims

Of madmen and children and demons
Transient souls
Raising the hair on my body
As they pass through.

CHILDHOOD

She was washed by the blood
And made whole
A thousand lambs sacrificed for the sins
Of one quiet girl alone in her room.

Pulling the shades cannot shut out
The cruel joy of her peers at play
Celebrating their existence as if it mattered
At half past three on a sunny day.

Running about as though
Their whole lives stretched before them
Caught in kinetic frenzy hardly
Electric enough to escape death or rain.

Heads filled with faces, horses, clowns,
Carnivalesque – surreal and frightening
A terrifying Ferris wheel you know
You could never get off alive.

A man going door-to-door to whom
Everyone must make themselves accountable
But she, waiting day after day, finally
Cannot remember what he wants.

DATING

Vipers! Who would poison your soul
Subjugate you under lovely smiles
Worn like watches, ticking on and on.

Sporting inevitability as their banner,
Hungry souls in a blaze of beauty
The fast trap, a whirlwind of terrible love.

Now innocence is no longer a virtue
And time is no longer on my side
And blood keeps spilling on my poems.

MADNESS

I don't want to leave my room it's dark in the hall
There are shadows that hang over me and reach out
I don't want to ride the bus I look in people's eyes
They stare with evil cruel intentions they despise me

I quit my job the people there were monsters behind masks –
I saw their gaping eyes try to catch me as I passed
Their flesh and fashion fantasy were thorough but still
I could see through the façade to their scaly skin beneath.

BRIAN

Ah Rome! The smell of sex and blood.
Papered with photographs of
Dead heroes and nameless faces.
Strange reproductive silhouettes.

Beads and chains and camouflage
Weapons on the bedroom wall.
Home of the people in negative
and neon boas.

The children who had to be killed
Because there weren't enough
Tickets to go around.
The nightmares – the terrors of day.

I created this world – you stay by choice
I knew you were the love of my life
When I saw the razors in your eyes
And your fingers burned through me like candles.

I KNOW WHO I AM

I would rather be a crow.
No pretension of soaring like an eagle
Or tasting freedom in the wind.

I should be content to perch
Atop a light pole next to my mate
Watching shiny cars go by
As though they existed solely for us.

No sweet melodies for me
I'd scream harshly with wisdom
Unburdened by all the needs of flesh.

I would hold no illusions
That I was special or unique
Happy to be one of many.

I'd know things then, see the big picture
Happy to chance upon
The dead squirrel, the trash lid unclosed.

Where the gulls nested
Content to steal an egg or two
Know which trees were heavy with fruit.

As the sun dropped in the sky
I'd call cordially to my friends
"See you at the murders!"

By dusk we'd all nestle in
Fluff up our feathers
And want nothing.

LOSS AND APATHY

I have waited here on this island
Until there was nothing left
To wait for.
All my heroes are dead now.

They've put them in boxes
And given them back to the earth
And the sea may sing
A song of mourning

But no one hears and no one cares.

All my heroes
Are dead now.

GRAY

Since you left
I am the color gray
Fallen from grace
A bird stripped of feathers
The sunset
Without color.

You took the green
From the trees.
The sky has no blue
The blue has no sky
Even the Black Lab
Has faded.

Your memory
Only shadows now.
Food has no flavor.
Waking and sleeping
There is no difference.

The moon still
Waxes and wanes
But it only signifies
The passing of time.
One more thing
We no longer share.

I am alone now
You took half
Of me with you
I kept the shell.

THE SUN WILL RISE

Just give me some time.

Maybe a year

To see myself clear.

I'll mail you an ear

In a plain

Brown envelope.

You can hold it to the wall

See if there's a message

Coming through

From the other side.

The bombs explode every day.

But love, only love

feels real in my hands

like stones or clamshells.

Not even death

Can convince me

That this is permanent.

THE SONG OF BEES

I brushed accidentally
Against the silver lace vine.

I heard the scurrying
Of dozens of bees, buzzing
And humming
Stirring the strands.
I sense their well-being
Their contentment.

The tiny white flowers, the
Golden bees, the leaves warm
And conscious of the sun.
I am not an intruder.
I am part of them.
I mean no harm.

The clouds hover
Their long white tendrils
Comfort me.
I have noticed
The moon still graces the sky.
I am finding peace.

CHICKENS

My hand is comforted
By the feel of this egg
Its perfect weight
The oval perfection seemingly
Made for the size and
Shape of my grasp.

Each hen's eggs are different
Identifiable by the size and color.

The chickens are crafty.
No dumb beasts here.

Snowflake has decided,
Against my objections
To jump up on the coop
Hop to the tree, the fence
Then into the neighbor's yard.
She has a nest under an agave.

Clearly
there are co-conspirators.

One day a pile of hay appears
On the nest. She goes
Every day, at nearly the same time
Then secretly deposits these brownish
Palm-perfect eggs. She knows
I cannot collect them there.

Yes, these chickens are clever.
But they do not
Keep secrets well.
As soon
As she lays the egg
A great clucking is heard.

The rooster runs to the fence
Followed by the other hens
a great collective
of clucking and crowing.
"It's an egg!
We have another one!"

I collect the others each day
But not a year passes
Without a secret nest somewhere,
Unfound, then suddenly
New life! The dogs fascinated
By cheeping of tiny chicks.

We watch in wonder
As they grow each day
Developing
their little chicken
Personalities, their colors
And patterns.

And praying all the while
"Please God, no roosters"

TICKING OFF THE HOURS

Spindling fingers
Weaving prayers
Throughout the day
The night.

Faceted rosary beads
Worn smooth
I am finding
My center again.

One bead at a time
I am coming
back together
bone by bone, vein by vein.

These prayers are
Binding my wounds
Stitching me up
Making me human again.

Giving me peace.

www.ingramcontent.com/pod-product-compliance
Lightning Source LLC
LaVergne TN
LVHW010506160826
845677LV00012B/2677
9798360886211